ABCs
OF FINGER
SPELLING

HANDY

Layout, Design-MICHAEL GEIGER
Illustration-NANCY BARTUSCH

Nancy Bartusch
B.F.A., M.A. in Fine Arts — University of Northern Iowa
M.F.A. in Design — University of Iowa
Freelance artist, have had several shows and won several art competitions. Really known for large acrylic - air brush paintings.

Michael Allen Geiger
Extensive training and hands on experience working with physically and mentally handicapped children and adults. Also experienced in crisis and drug abuse counseling.

Dedicated to — Marie B.

A a

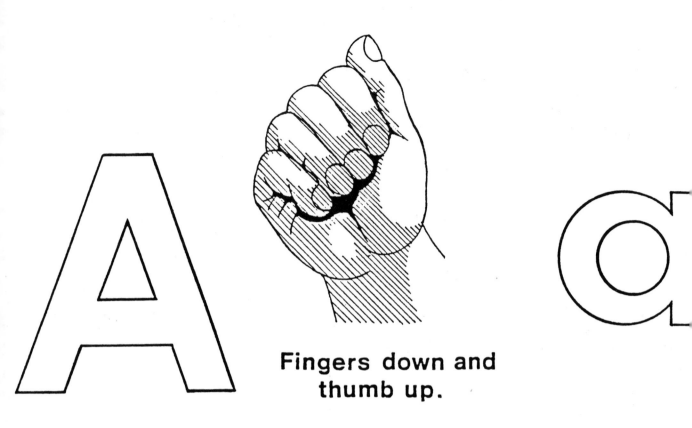

Fingers down and thumb up.

APPLE

Twist sign for X on chee

Apple

B 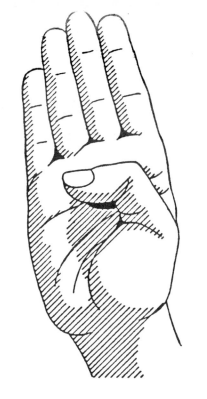 b

All fingers up.
Thumb down.

BOAT

Put flat hands
together at little
fingers. Move the
forward with a wa
up-down motion.

Boat

**Fingers curved together.
Thumb out.**

CLOWN

**Claw shaped [...]
shakes in fro[...]
of nose.**

Clown

D d

Touch second finger with thumb.

Both A-hands drum alternatel

Drum

Thumb touches finger tips.

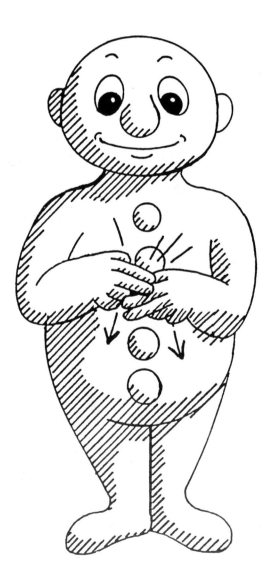

Right H breaks on the left H and separates downward.

Egg

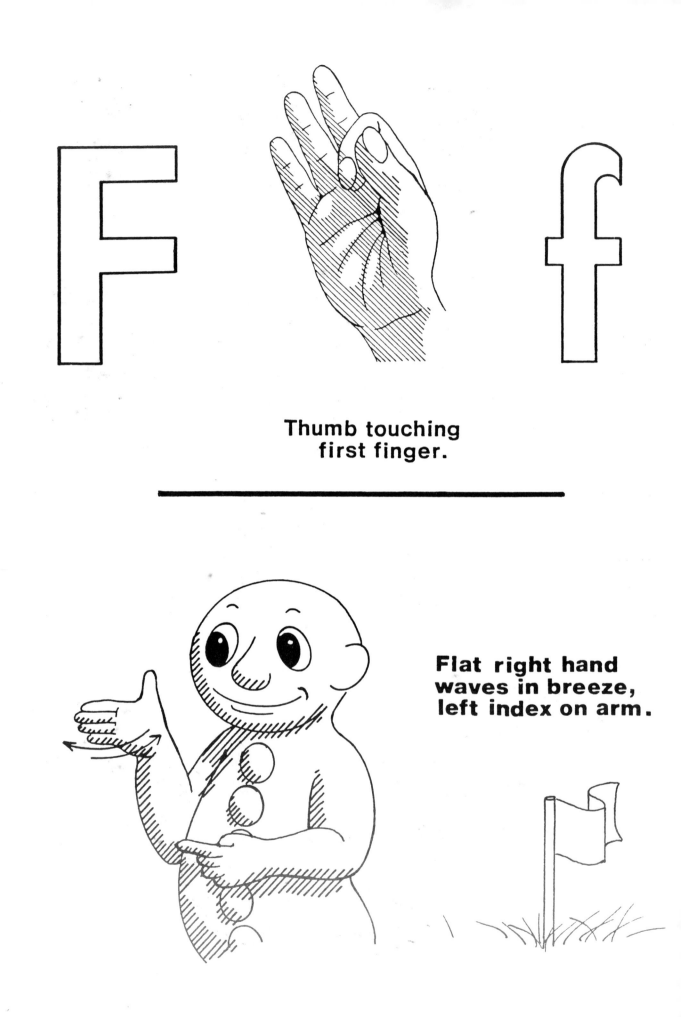

F f

**Thumb touching
first finger.**

**Flat right hand
waves in breeze,
left index on arm.**

**Point with
first finger and thumb.**

___

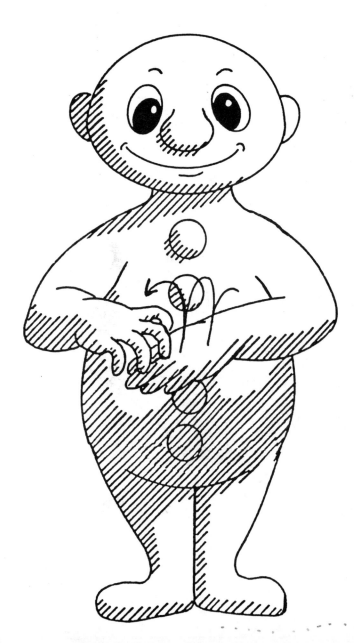

**Fingers of right
claw-hand hop across
back of left hand.**

Add S —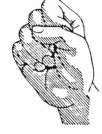

Grapes

H h

Point with first
two fingers.

Flat palms outlin[e]
roof and sides.

House

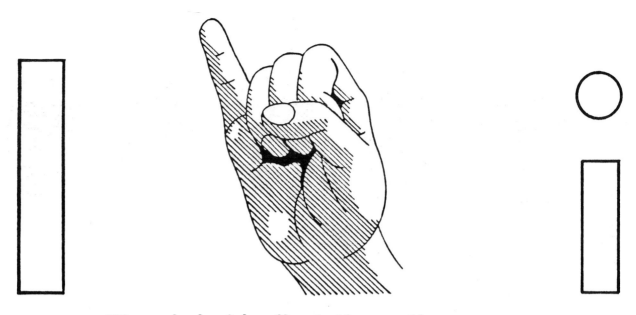

Thumb holds first three fingers.

Sign F at side of mouth, then on cheek in front of ear.

Indian

J j

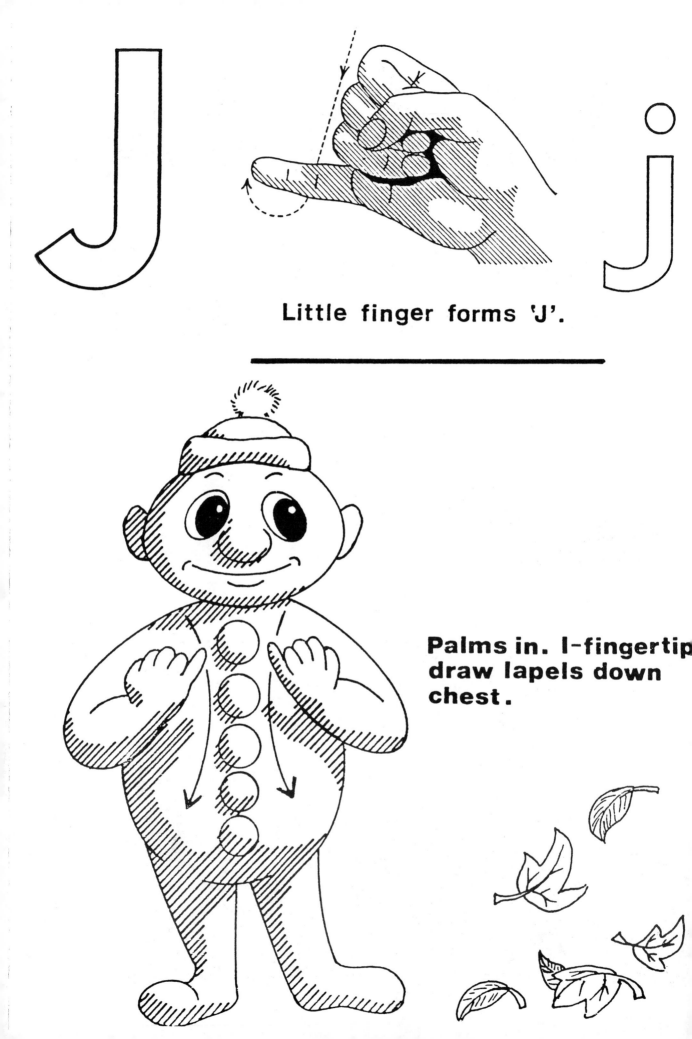

Little finger forms 'J'.

Palms in. I-fingertips
draw lapels down
chest.

Jacket

K   k

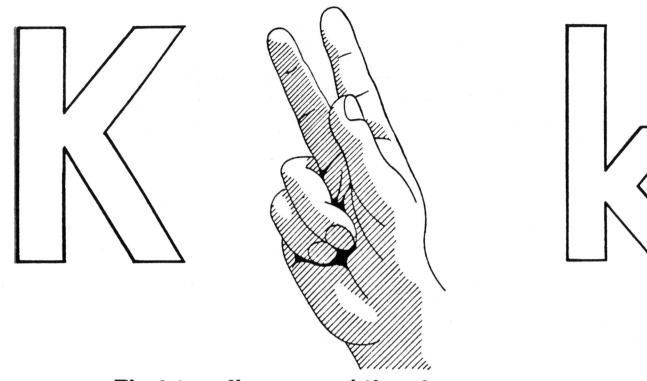

First two fingers and thumb up.
Second finger forward with thumb touching.

Palm-out K moves upward in wavy motion.

Kite

L

First finger up and thumb out.

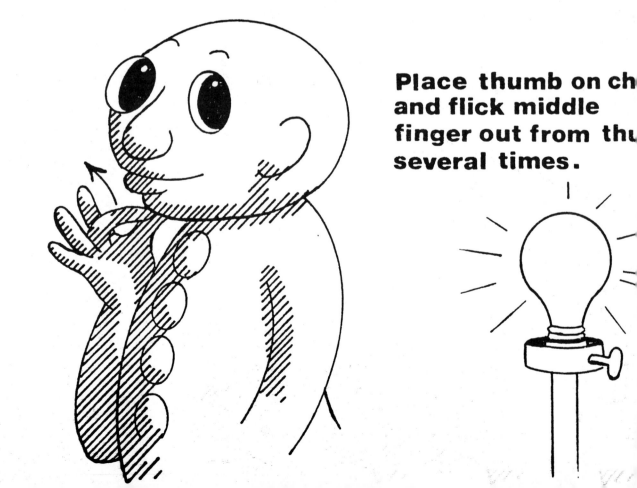

**Place thumb on ch
and flick middle
finger out from thu
several times.**

Lamp

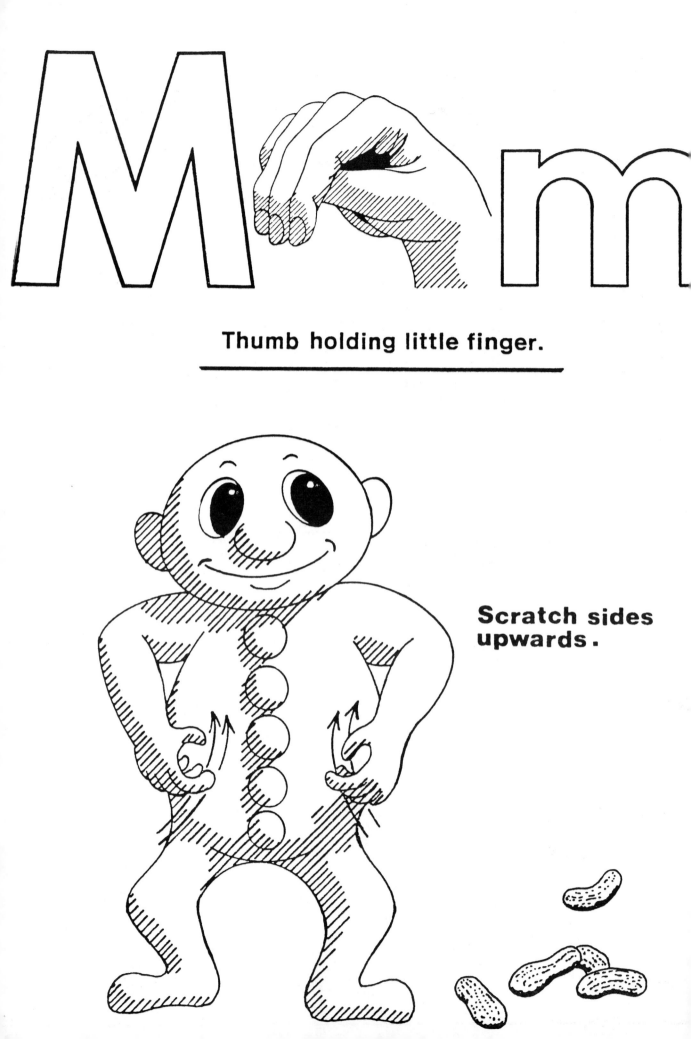

M m

Thumb holding little finger.

Scratch sides upwards.

Monkey

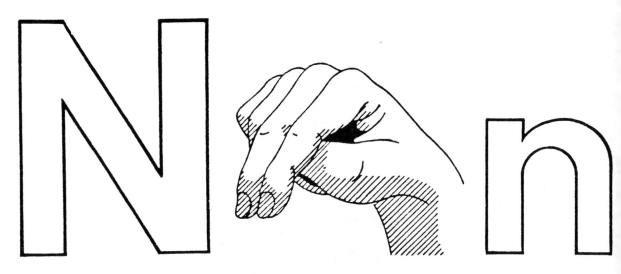

**Hold last two fingers
with thumb.**

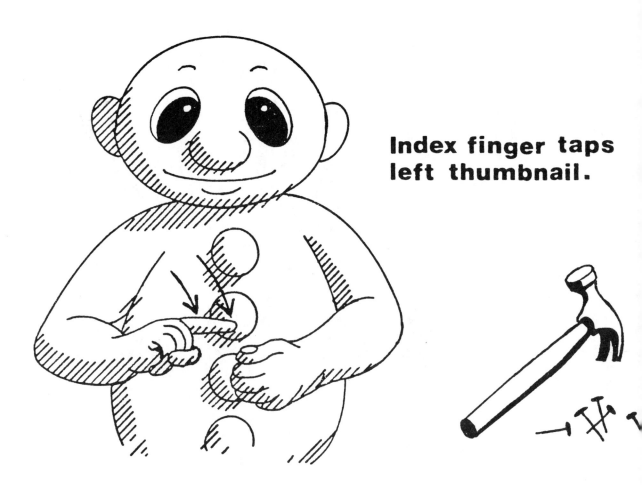

**Index finger taps
left thumbnail.**

Nail

and

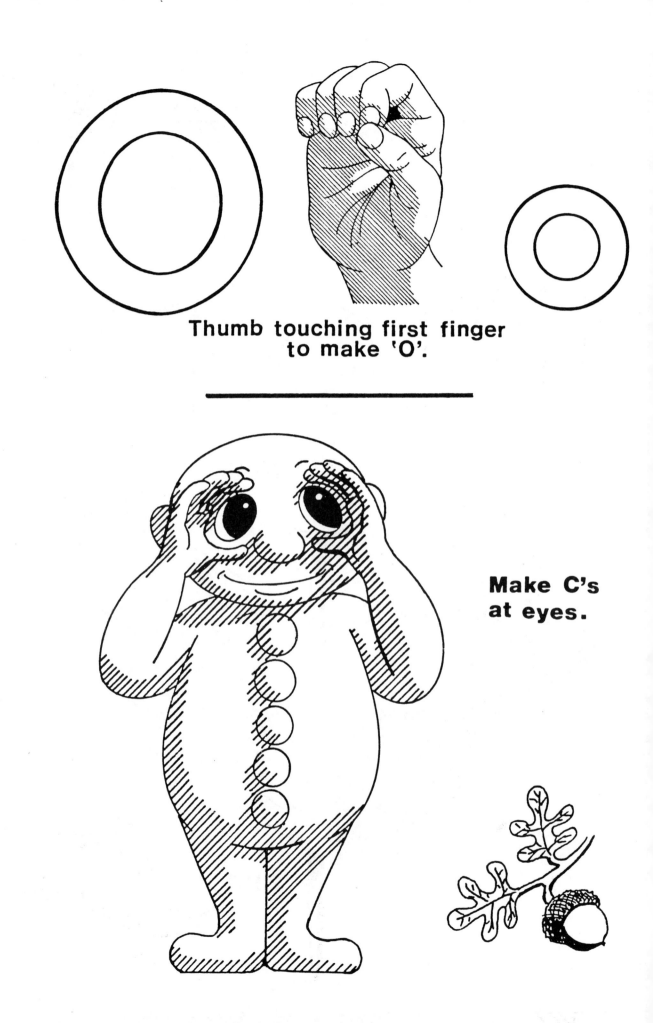

**Thumb touching first finger
to make 'O'.**

**Make C's
at eyes.**

Owl

P p

Point with first finger.
Second finger down touching thumb.

Fingers together,
hand flaps under
chin.

Pig

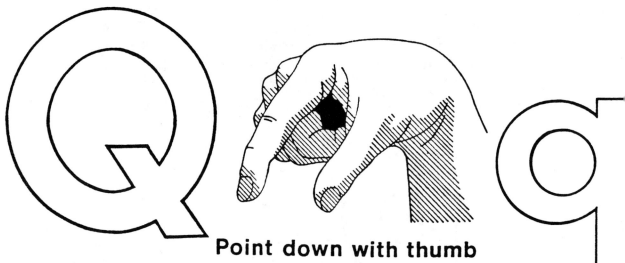

Point down with thumb and first finger.

Right Q on left shoulder, moves down to right waist.

Queen

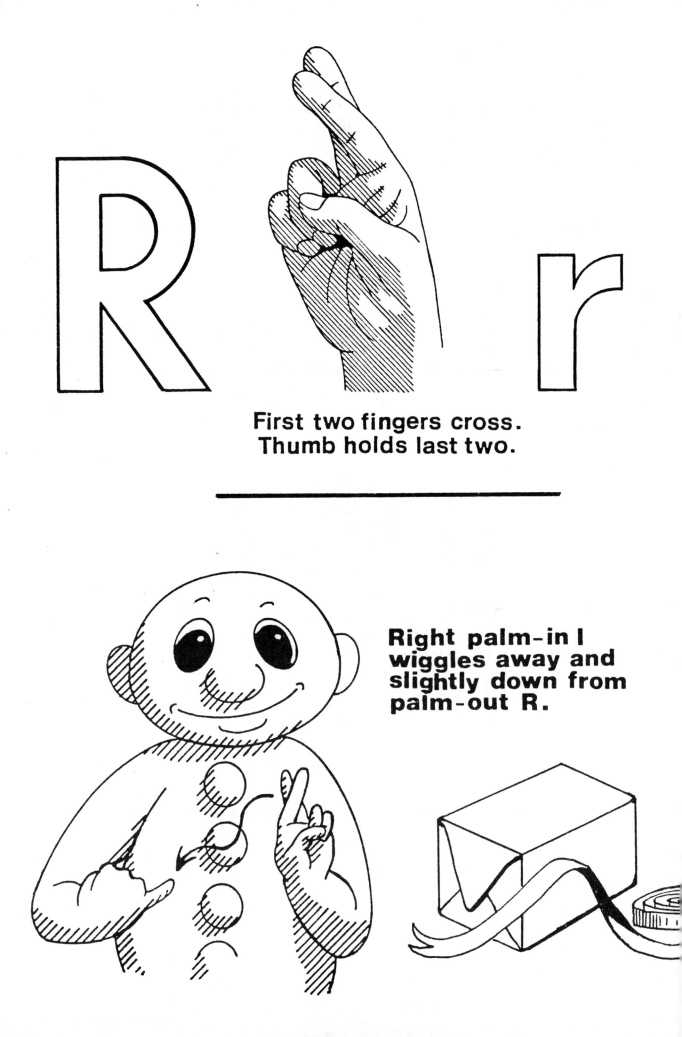

R **r**

First two fingers cross.
Thumb holds last two.

Right palm-in I
wiggles away and
slightly down from
palm-out R.

Ribbon

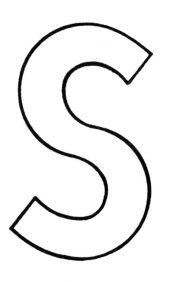 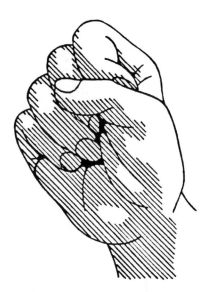 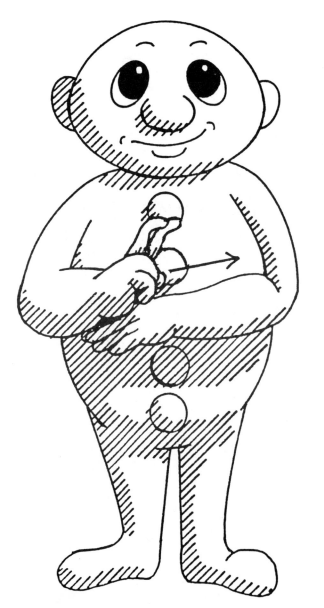

**Make a fist.
Thumb outside.**

**Heel of bent–V
slides up left
forearm.**

T T t

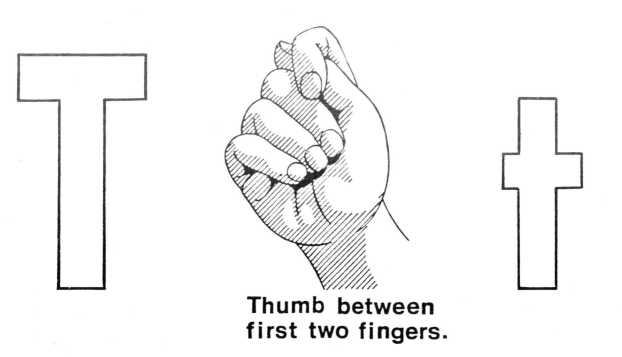

**Thumb between
first two fingers.**

**Left hand covers
right palm-left A;
wiggle right thumb.**

Turtle

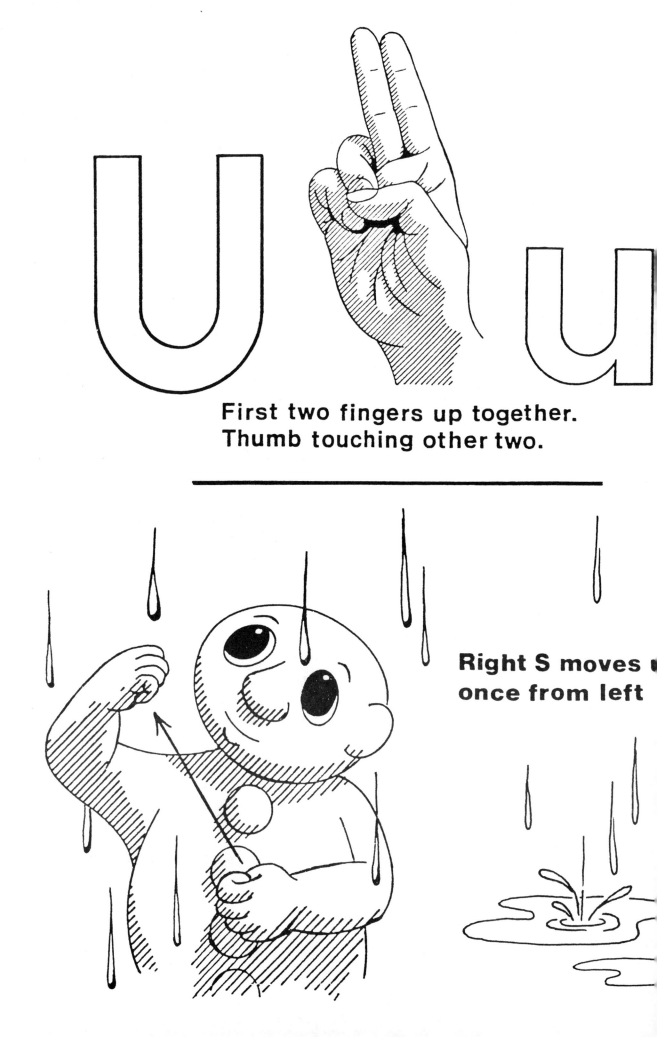

First two fingers up together.
Thumb touching other two.

Right S moves
once from left

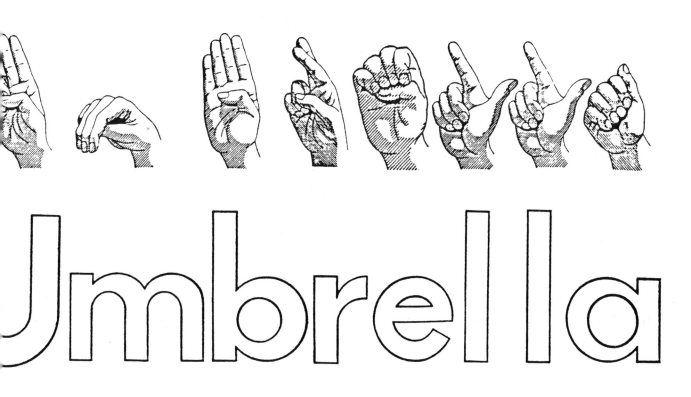

Umbrella

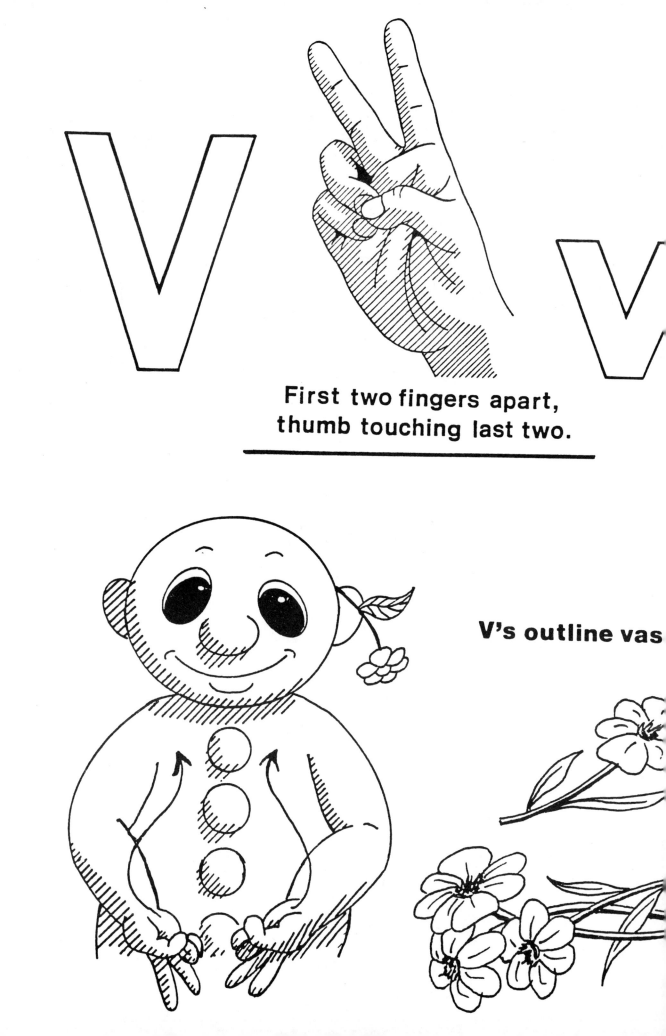

First two fingers apart,
thumb touching last two.

V's outline vas

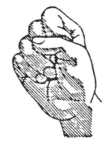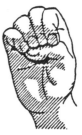

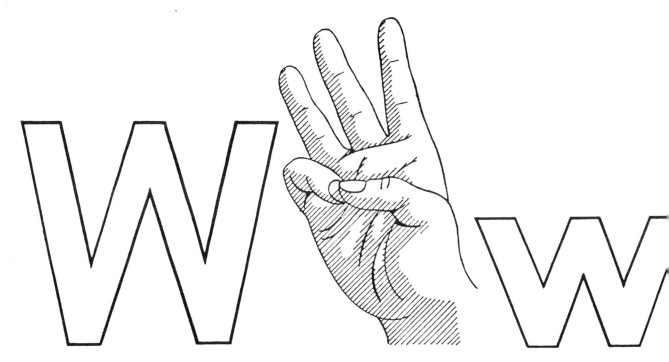

**Thumb touches little finger.
Other three fingers up and apart.**

**W-hands face each
other and drop
straight down.**

X x

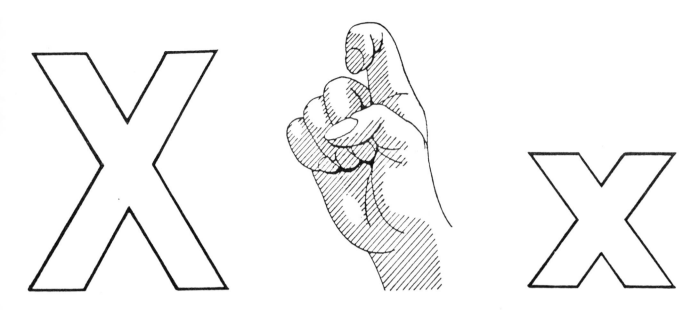

**First finger out and bent.
Thumb over last three fingers.**

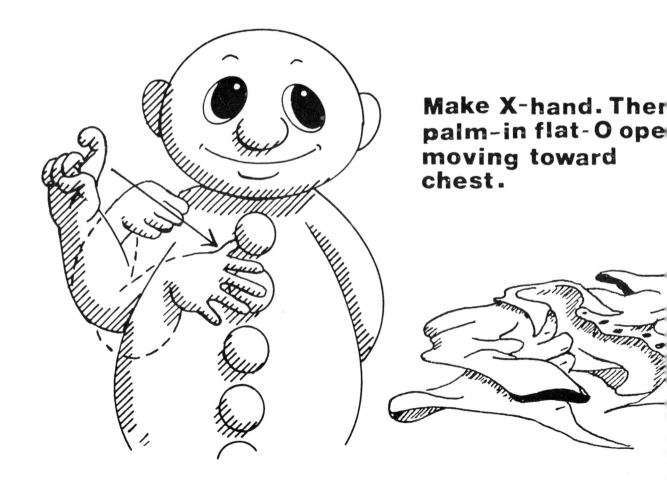

**Make X-hand. Ther
palm-in flat-O ope
moving toward
chest.**

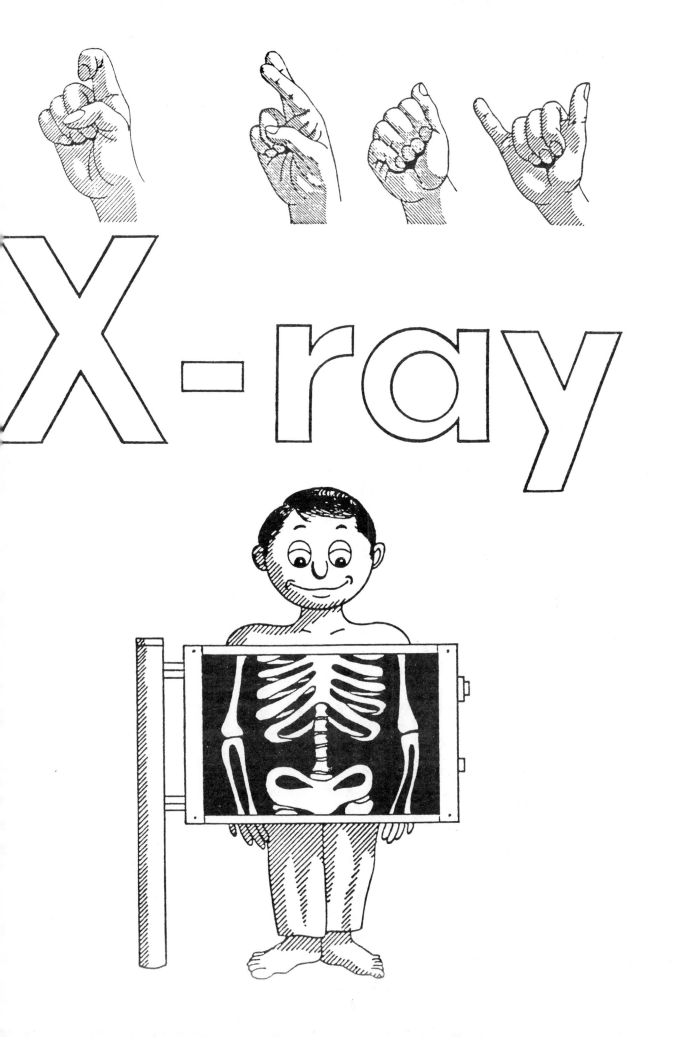

X-ray

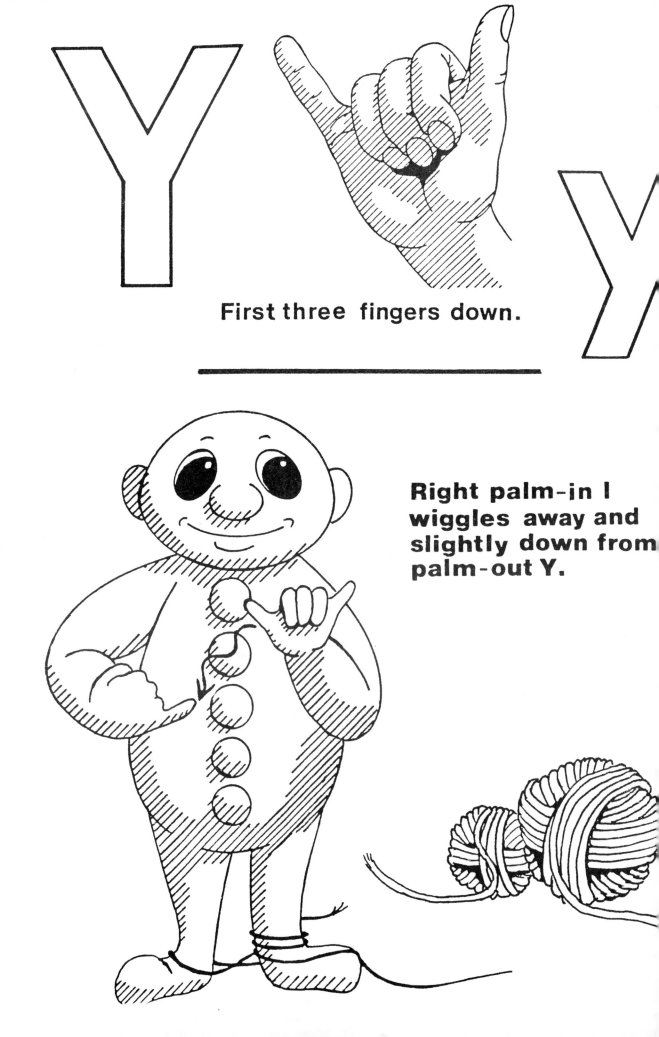

Y

First three fingers down.

Right palm-in I wiggles away and slightly down from palm-out Y.

Yarn

Z

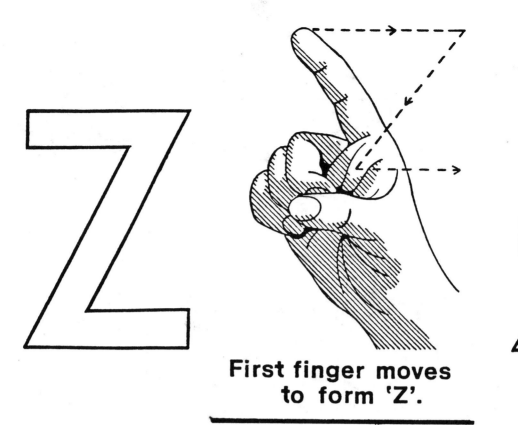

First finger moves to form 'Z'.

4–hands mar
stripes on bo

4-hand

Zebra

OTHER PRODUCTS from
MODERN SIGNS PRESS, INC.

Basic Tools and Techniques
Teaching and Learning Signing Exact English
Student Workbook

Video Tapes
Curriculum Tapes
Beginning level – 14 lessons
Rather Strange Stories (Intermediate level)

Visual Tales (available in Signed English or ASL)
The Father, The Son and The Donkey
Village Stew
The Greedy Cat
The Magic Pot
The House That Jack Built

Signed Cartoons (available in Signed English or ASL)

Three Pigs	Three Bears	Casper	Animal Antics
Popeye	Raggedy Ann	Superman	Shipshape Shapes
Rudolph	Elmer & Bugs	Cinderella	Numbers
Daffy Duck	Bugs Bunny	Felix the Cat	

Show and Tell Stories
Series 1 – Brown Bear, Brown Bear...; and, This Is Me

Informational Tapes
Deafness the Hidden Handicap
Growing Up with SEE

Children's Collection
Coloring Books
ABC's of Fingerspelling
Sign Numbers

Storybooks
Talking Finger Series - Popsicles are Cold, At Grandma's House,
Little Green Monsters, I was So Mad
Jean's Christmas Stocking
In Our House
Be Happy Not Sad (two books including coloring workbook)
Grandfather Moose (finger rhymes)
Cosmo Gets An Ear